The Truth Revealed

Ḥaḍrat Mirza Ghulam Ahmad
of Qadian[as]
The Promised Messiah and Mahdi
Founder of the Ahmadiyya Muslim Jamāʻat

ISLAM INTERNATIONAL PUBLICATIONS LIMITED

The Truth Revealed
English translation of
Sachchā'ī kā Iẓhār (Urdu)
by Ḥaḍrat Mirza Ghulam Ahmad of Qadian,
the Promised Messiah and Mahdi[as].

© Islam International Publications Ltd.

First Edition (Urdu): 1893
English Edition: UK 2010

Published by:
    Islam International Publications Ltd.
    'Islamabad' Sheephatch Lane,
    Tilford, Surrey GU10 2AQ
    United Kingdom

Printed in UK at:
    Raqeem Press
    'Islamabad'
    Tilford, Surrey GU10 2AQ

ISBN: 978-1-84880-054-0

Contents

Introduction v

Publishers' Note vii

A Narrative of the Help Received by the Christian Clergy Regarding Certain Theological Matters from Shaikh Muḥammad Ḥussain Batālwī Sahib's Ishā'atus-Sunnah 1

A General Notice 5

The Removal of a Misgiving Harboured by Dr. Martyn Clarke 7

A Loving Letter Written to me by an Arab Scholar 9

My Response to this Heartfelt Correspondence 11

An Arab Scholar's letter from Mecca 13

An Excerpt from a Letter Written by an Arab Scholar, Sayyed 'Alī, Son of Sharīf Muṣṭafā 14

A Promise by Mr. 'Abdullāh Ātham, Representative of Dr. Martyn Clarke and the Christians, to Accept Islam if he is Defeated 17

A Copy of the Letter Written by Mr. 'Abdullāh Ātham on 9 May 1893 from Amritsar 17

A Mubāhalah Invitation in Response to the Announcement Published by 'Abdul Ḥaq Ghaznavī 19

بِسْمِ اللّٰهِ الرَّحْمٰنِ الرَّحِيْمِ

Introduction

About the Author

Born in 1835 in Qadian (India), Ḥaḍrat Mirza Ghulam Ahmad, the Promised Messiah and Mahdi[as], devoted himself to the study of the Holy Quran and to a life of prayer and contemplation. Finding Islam the target of theological attacks and the fortunes of Muslims at a low ebb, he undertook the vindication and exposition of Islam. In his vast corpus of writings (including the epoch-making *Barāhīn-e-Ahmadiyyah*), his lectures, discourses, religious debates etc., he argued that Islam was a living faith and the only religion capable of establishing a relationship with man and his creator. The teachings contained in the Holy Quran and the Law promulgated by Islam were designed to raise man to moral, intellectual and spiritual perfection. He announced that God had appointed him the Messiah and Mahdi as mentioned in the prophecies of the Bible, the Holy Quran and Hadith. In 1889 he began to accept initiation into the Ahmadiyya Jamā'at, which is now established in almost two hundred countries. His eighty books are written mostly in Urdu, but a significant proportion of his writings are also in Arabic and Persian.

About the Book

Published by the Promised Messiah[as] in May 1893, *Sachchā'ī kā Iẓhār* [*The Truth Revealed*] is a short collection of letters, articles, and public announcements set amidst the backdrop of the well-

Introduction

known debate between the Promised Messiah[as] and the Christian missionary 'Abdullāh Ātham, the proceedings of which were published in the book *Jang-e-Muqaddas*.

Acknowledgments

I would like to express my appreciation for the help and support given by Maulana Muniruddin Shams Sahib, Additional Wakīlut Taṣnīf, London and Dr. Muhammad Shafiq Sehgal Sahib, for their valuable suggestions and their help in bringing out this book.

I owe a debt of gratitude to the following who worked diligently in the various stages of this translation: Mirza Usman Ahmad Adam, Raja Ata-ul-Mannan, Tahir Mahmood Mubashar and Syed Tanwir Mujtaba.

Chaudhary Muhammad Ali
Wakīlut-Taṣnīf
Rabwah
1 June 2010

Publishers' Note

The words in the text in normal brackets () and in between the long dashes—are the words of the Promised Messiah[as] and if any explanatory words or phrases are added by the translator for the purpose of clarification, they are put in square brackets [ ].

The name of Muhammad[sa], the Holy Prophet of Islam, has been followed by the symbol [sa], which is an abbreviation for the salutation *Ṣallallāhu 'Alaihi Wasallam* (may peace and blessings of Allah be upon him). The names of other Prophets and Messengers are followed by the symbol [as], an abbreviation for *'Alaihissalām* (on whom be peace). The actual salutations have not generally been set out in full, but they should nevertheless, be understood as being repeated in full in each case. The symbol [ra] is used with the name of the companions of the Holy Prophet[sa] and those of the Promised Messiah[as]. It stands for *Raḍi Allāhu 'anhu/'anhā/'anhum* (May Allah be pleased with him/with her/with them). [rh] stands for *Raḥimahullāhu Ta'ālā* (may Allah have mercy on him). [at] stands for *Ayyadahullāhu Ta'ālā* (May Allah, the Mighty help him).

In transliterating Arabic words we have followed the following system adopted by the Royal Asiatic Society.

ا	at the beginning of a word, pronounced as *a*, *i*, *u* preceded by a very slight aspiration, like *h* in the English word 'honour'.
ث	*th*, pronounced like th in the English word 'thing'.

Publishers' Note

ح	*ḥ*, a guttural aspirate, stronger than h.
خ	*kh*, pronounced like the Scotch ch in 'loch'.
ذ	*dh*, pronounced like the English th in 'that'.
ص	*ṣ*, strongly articulated s.
ض	*ḍ*, similar to the English th in 'this'.
ط	*ṭ*, strongly articulated palatal t.
ظ	*ẓ*, strongly articulated z.
ع	ʿ, a strong guttural, the pronunciation of which must be learnt by the ear.
غ	*gh*, a sound approached very nearly in the r '*grasseye*' in French, and in the German r. It requires the muscles of the throat to be in the 'gargling' position whilst pronouncing it.
ق	*q*, a deep guttural k sound.
ى	ʾ, a sort of catch in the voice.

Short vowels are represented by:

a for ─َ─ (like *u* in 'bud');
i for ─ِ─ (like *i* in 'bid');
u for ─ُ─ (like *oo* in 'wood');

Long vowels by:

ā for ─ا─ or آ (like *a* in 'father');
ī for ى ─ِ─ or ─ِى─ (like *ee* in 'deep');
ū for و ─ُ─ (like *oo* in 'root');

Other:

ai for ى ─َ─ (like *i* in 'site')*;
au for و ─َ─ (resembling *ou* in 'sound').

Please note that in transliterated words the letter 'e' is to be pronounced as in 'prey' which rhymes with 'day'; however the

---

*In Arabic words like شيخ (Shaikh) there is an element of diphthong which is missing when the word is pronounced in Urdu.

Publishers' Note

pronunciation is flat without the element of English diphthong. If in Urdu and Persian words 'e' is lengthened a bit more it is transliterated as 'ei' to be pronounced as 'ei' in 'feign' without the element of diphthong thus 'کے' is transliterated as 'Kei'. For the nasal sound of 'n' we have used the symbol 'ń'. Thus Urdu word 'میں' is transliterated as 'meiń'.*

The consonants not included in the above list have the same phonetic value as in the principal languages of Europe.

We have not transliterated Arabic words which have become part of the English language, e.g., Islam, Mahdi, Quran**, Hijra, Ramadan, Hadith, ulema, umma, sunna, kafir, pukka etc.

For quotes straight commas (straight quotes) are used to differentiate them from the curved commas used in the system of transliteration, ' for ع, ' for ء. Commas as punctuation marks are used according to the normal usage. Similarly for apostrophe normal usage is followed.

---

* These transliterations are not included in the system of transliteration by Royal Asiatic Society. [Publishers]

** Concise Oxford Dictionary records Quran in three forms—Quran, Qur'an and Koran. [Publishers]

بِسْمِ اللهِ الرَّحْمٰنِ الرَّحِيْمِ

نَحْمَدُهٗ وَنُصَلِّىْ عَلٰى رَسُوْلِهِ الْكَرِيْمِ[1]

A Narrative of the Help Received by the Christian Clergy Regarding Certain Theological Matters from Shaikh Muḥammad Ḥussain Batālwī Sahib's *Ishāʻatus-Sunnah*

The American Mission Press, Ludhiana, recently published a disparaging advertisement about me on behalf of Dr. Henry Martyn Clarke M.D. the medical missionary of Amritsar on 12 May, 1893. This announcement was, in a sense, also an expression of gratitude to the renowned Maulawī Shaikh Muḥammad Ḥussain of Batala. The Christians were indeed beholden to him for the following reason: Dr. Clarke had agreed to meet me in a debate in order to inquire into Islam and Christianity and distinguish truth from falsehood. But after ruminating over his decision he was greatly perturbed. This was perhaps hardly surprising; in truth, when a doctrine like the one of taking a mortal for a God is closely scrutinised, its adherents always experience convulsions. God is God and man is man. What likeness do dust and ash have with the Holy and Omnipotent Lord? Thus the clergy were disquieted, lest the falsity

---

[1] In the name of Allah, the Gracious, the Merciful. We praise Allah and invoke His blessings upon His noble Messenger[sa].

[Publishers]

of their faith be exposed by the perfect teaching of Islam. It was better for them to postpone our contest and have this poisoned chalice dashed from their lips. So, in the hour of their despair they were ably assisted by Shaikh Sahib. One may assume that he himself approached them surreptitiously. I have drawn this inference on the basis of a letter sent to me by Dr. Clarke in which he has reproduced arguments from *Ishā'atus-Sunnah* and his discourse bears a striking resemblance to that of Shaikh Sahib's. I am confident that, if asked to swear an oath, Shaikh Sahib would not deny his involvement. This assumption is given further credence by [the aforementioned] advertisement issued in the *Nūr Afshāń* of 12 May 1893 in the form of a supplement which I too have a copy of. It is as follows:

> You (the residents of Jandiala) have chosen as your representative for the debate an individual (i.e., myself) who can scarcely be considered a Muhammadan. How could you have made such a grave error? Have you not read the edicts issued against Mirza Ghulam Ahmad of Qadian by the Muslim ulema of India and the Punjab (here Dr. Clarke reproduces these edicts): "All the answers we have given the questioner and all that we have decreed with regards to the Qadiani is correct and can be verified by the Quran, the practice of the Prophet and the sayings of the ulema. It is incumbent on all the Muslims to shun this Dajjāl and impostor and not to engage him in any religious practices that are common among the Muslims. They must

not seek his companionship, extend to him the greeting of peace, invite him or accept his invitation to traditional Islamic ceremonies, pray behind him or observe his funeral prayer. He is like a virus that afflicts the faith. He is a Dajjāl, an impostor, accursed, a heretic, outside the pale of Islam, a disbeliever, nay the most foul disbeliever, wily, deceived by Satan and the deceiver of others, banished from the Sunnah and the Muslim community, the greatest Dajjāl and one who uses religion to feed his material appetite." For a full account one can procure a copy of *Ishā'atus-Sunnah* by Maulawī Abū Sa'īd Muhammad Hussain Sahib at a cost of 1 rupee and 50 paisas from Lahore. That you have overlooked this tract is indeed mystifying. Bravo! You and the people of Jandiala have committed a grave affront by choosing as your religious leader one whose funeral prayer cannot even be observed. How could you have been so deceived?

It would be worthwhile to consider how the cleric may have profited from Batālwī Sahib and his *Ishā'atus-Sunnah* and indeed how my other opponents may also have benefitted from this affair. [But before turning to this, I would like] to express my satisfaction at the fact that when the devoted people of Jandiala read this pernicious letter their resolve did not falter and Miāṅ Muhammad Bukhsh Sahib gave the Christians a stirring riposte arguing that no faith, including Christianity, was free from internecine disputes. He further retorted that he regarded as mischief makers those maulawīs who denounce a champion of Islam as a disbeliever.

A General Notice

Twice did Shaikh Batālwī Sahib, author of *Ishā'atus-Sunnah,* swear a solemn oath that he would, by a certain date, reply to my letter regarding the writing of an Arabic commentary and *Qaṣīdah*. 16 days have elapsed on both his promises. God knows how many more will pass. Shaikh Sahib's promises and his breaking of them clearly suggest that he finds himself in a quandary.

Three days ago, I received a rather terse message from the maulawīs of Amritsar that if I am to debate Dr. Clarke on the life and death of Jesus they will most certainly presume to side with him. Thus, I give a general notice to Shaikh Sahib and his ilk, nay, I challenge them to do all that is in their power, for I will assuredly debate Dr. Clarke on this matter. They are at full liberty to assist him in any way if they should so desire.

وَاعْلَمُوْا اَنَّ اللّٰهَ یُخْزِی الْکَاذِبِیْنَ ـ وَاٰخِرُ دَعْوَانَا اَنِ الْحَمْدُ لِلّٰهِ رَبِّ الْعَالَمِیْنَ ـ[2]

---

[2] Know, that God will assuredly bring disgrace upon the liars. And all praise belongs to Allah, the Lord of the worlds.

[Publishers]

The Removal of a Misgiving Harboured by Dr. Martyn Clarke

It seems good logic to reason from the announcement published in a supplement of the *Nūr Afshāṅ* on 12 May 1893 that either Dr. Clarke has been taken in by the Shaikh's contention that Islam's recognized ulema have declared me an apostate, or that he himself wishes to mislead others. Therefore, to apprise the people, I deem it necessary to write that those ulema who are blessed with the knowledge and practice of religion and have been bestowed with the light of faith are with me and they are almost forty in number. The converse is true of the maulawīs aligned with my opponents who are maulawīs in name alone and are devoid of practical and scholarly excellences. If Dr. Clarke considers this a hyperbole, he should attend a gathering or a debate between those ulema who oppose me and those who follow me so as to formulate a fair and just opinion. Indeed, not long from now, on 15 June, 1893 such a debate is scheduled between one of my opponents, Maulawī Ghulām Dastagīr, and with him the ulema of Lahore who share his temper and disposition, and a small number of my learned followers. Then the clergyman [Dr. Clarke] can judge for himself on which side of the divide stand the righteous and distinguished ulema and on which side stand those who carry the title of maulawī but are in actual fact inarticulate and nescient. As the old adage has it, seeing is believing. The partisan discourses of our miserly opponents are looked on with disdain by learned eyes. Truth is only manifested after being subjected to scrutiny.

Dr. Clarke is well aware that Mecca and Medina are home to Islam's most distinguished ulema and are thus the cradles of Islamic learning. *My Allah increase both Holy sites in glory, honour and grace.* So in the very depths of these sacred cities reside such ulema who have joined me. By way of example, I have instanced three letters written to me by or with reference to such eminent personalities.

(The first of these letters speaks of the profound impression made on an Arab scholar by my book *Ā'īna-e-Kamālāt-e-Islam* and in particular the section entitled *Tablīgh*. The gentleman in question teaches literature at one of the great institutions of the Arab world)

My respected brother Maulawī Ḥāfiẓ Muḥammad Ya'qūb Sahib writes from Dehra Dun:

> I believe that you are the Imam of the age and one supported by God. No doubt, God will subjugate the ulema and make them your servants. Their efforts to oppose you will yield them no reward. I yearn for Allah to allow me to live and die as your servant. Lord! Let it come to pass. [As I write this] I am with an Arab scholar. He is from Syria, he is a Sayyed and a prodigious writer who has memorised many of the treasures of ancient Arabic verse. We spoke of you at great length. I, who am just a simple man, presented your

interpretation of the word *tawaffā* before this erudite authority on Arabic. How he was dumbfounded! I showed him an excerpt from your Arabic work *Ā'ina-e-Kamālāt-e-Islam*. He was overawed by the beauty of its prose and exclaimed that no Arab could write this eloquently, much less an Indian. I gave him your *Qaṣīdah* which drew tears from his eyes. As he read it he lamented the impoverished state of contemporary Arabic verse and swore an oath to the Lord that he would commit your poetry to memory. Then my learned friend exclaimed that even if an Arab were to claim to be your equal he would be like the false-prophet Musailmah. Thus ended our discussion. I am convinced that what you say is from the Lord and a miraculous sign of His support. Your words cannot have their origins in the imaginings of man. I hereby make you master over my life, property and children.

A Loving Letter Written to me by an Arab Scholar

In the name of Allah, the Gracious, the Merciful.

The morning breeze whispers eulogies of your excellences; your being emits the scent of the sweetest flowers; your greatness remains concealed from the eyes of the people; you have been saved from the evils of fate; may the ships of your salvation always sail across the uncertain waters of knowledge and learning; may you confront the subtleties of understanding; may people submit to your greatness and be witness to your ineffable virtues. I cannot summon the words to praise you, to pray for you, to speak of my longing to meet you.

May the peace and blessings of Allah be upon you.

This letter is a token of love from one whose heart is pure. A flame was once kindled in my heart that ignited an insatiable passion for travel and adventure, so I left my native land and destiny brought me here and the Will of God decreed that I meet with my kindly brother Ḥāfiẓ Maulawī Muḥammad Yaʻqūb. May the Lord protect him from all that is impure and from the innumerable vices prevalent in the town of Dehra Dun. We spoke of recent events and indulged in tales and stories of the past, and then your name was mentioned. I inquired about you at length and he told me of your unequalled etiquette and civility. After hearing of the beauty of your character, I was drawn towards you and desired to see you for myself; after all, the virtues of the speaker are reflected by his words. To meet someone face to face has its own benefits, hence Moses' prayer [to see God for himself]. But my path to you is thwarted by the rigours of travel, the extremity of the summer heat, my pennilessness and a lack of conveyance.

> *Could I take to the air*
> *I would soar to you in all haste*
> *Alas, my wings have been cut*
> *And a bird without wings cannot fly.*

Nonetheless, if I cannot come to you in person I can at

least write. As the proverb says, the letter is half a meeting. To merely be aware of a thing is not to know it; only experience can give birth to belief and conviction. And so one has to make do with what one has.

My Response to this Heartfelt Correspondence

بِسْمِ اللّٰهِ الرَّحْمٰنِ الرَّحِيْمِ
نَحْمَدُهٗ وَنُصَلِّيْ عَلٰى رَسُوْلِهِ الْكَرِيْمِ[3]

May the peace and blessings of Allah be upon you.

My dear, who loves me and is sincere to me, I received your affectionate letter. As I read it, I perceived it to be written by one who is true, righteous, learned, intelligent, perceptive and bestowed by the All-Seeing Lord to me who has been preyed on as a disbeliever and rejected by all.

So, I thanked Allah for making you a source of solace for me. He has revealed that I will be loved by the virtuous. I have written a book for the honoured peoples of Arabia and Syria so that they may come to my aid. Your letter arrived during these blessed days [that is, as I wrote this work]. Thus I assumed you to be the first of the blossoming fruit and an omen of the coming reformation of the East and the West. In my heart I longed for God to take me to your land so that mine

---

[3] In the name of Allah, the Gracious, the Merciful. We praise Allah and invoke His blessings upon His noble Messenger[sa].

[Publishers]

eyes might look upon you.

My brother! The ulema of my country call me a disbeliever, reject me and impute all manner of foul things. Time and again I have expressed my revulsion for them and their self-professed knowledge. I am among those who doubt their faith. I perceive their hearts to be like those Jews who succumbed to ill thoughts and showed impertinence before the Lord Who is worthy of worship. They persist in calling me a liar and have made every effort to hurt and offend me. Their discourses and addresses denounce one who is believer in the unity of God as a heretic and they are not ashamed of their impetuousness. Do they not understand that the time has come for the revival of the faith and the advent of the reformer who is to defeat Satan? Do they not see the spread of darkness, the cloud of uncertainty that obscures the path of rightness, the enemies of Islam besieging the religion and light having given way to darkness?

A people have arisen who worship the cross and take as their Lord a mere mortal. All are led astray by them and they possess nothing but lies, deception and material wealth. The blind are drawn towards them and people upon people are ensnared by their falsehood. It is possible that many Muslims may be destroyed at the hands of these deceivers.

Allah found this people [the Muslims] succumbed to weakness, so He sent one from among His servants to revive the faith and bring them victory.

My brother! A long night has settled over Islam and the right path lies untraveled. When Allah looked on the darkness of this evil and the mischief, disbelief and transgression of this age, He found the people standing on the brink of fire. So He gave to them a light from Himself to save them from this deception and to show them His signs and lead them to the right path.

I have related to you the weight of my woes so that you too may grieve over the plight of Islam, for I perceive that you are a righteous young gentleman, sincere and devoted. The love imbued in your words has gladdened the heart of one who has been rejected and reviled by his people.

May Allah reward you in turn, and have mercy on you, for He is most Merciful.

Mirza Ghulam Ahmad

An Arab Scholar's letter from Mecca

In the name of Allah, the Gracious, the Merciful

All praise belongs to Allah, Lord of all the worlds. Peace be upon the Holy Prophet[sa], the greatest of His servants.

Dearly honoured and esteemed master, our guide and Messiah, Ḥaḍrat Mirza Ghulam Ahmad. May God protect you. Amen. May the peace and blessings of Allah be upon you.

I received your loving letter and read it carefully, all the while thanking God that you were well. I seek forgiveness of Allah and of you for the error of my ways. I am your son and servant and answerable to the Lord and to you. I promise, God willing, I will not be guilty of the same error again. May Allah better your situation and shower you with His rewards and blessings.

Muḥammad bin Aḥmad Makkī

I was greatly moved by what you have written in your book. All praise belongs to Allah Who has promised me a meeting with you. There is no doubt that you have been sent by God. I have believed in you and considered you to be true and say once again that all praise belongs to Allah, Lord of all the worlds.

Muḥammad bin Aḥmad Makkī

An Excerpt from a Letter Written by an Arab Scholar, Sayyed 'Alī, Son of Sharīf Muṣṭafā

Sayyed Sahib from Arabia wrote me a lengthy correspondence abounding in verses of *Qaṣīdah* and passages of prose written in praise and laudation. The following is an excerpt of his letter:

Dear Mirza Ghulam Ahmad

My salutations to you, who are wise, enlightened, learned, the star of the East, a Messenger of the Lord and the recipient of His revelation, a pillar in the eternal sultanate of Islam and the King of the Muslims.

Your excellences are like the stars that illuminate the night sky. They are there for all to see. You are an endless ocean of generosity and munificence and a clear fountain of knowledge and learning.

I may publish all the verses of the *Qaṣīdah* and the full letter written by this Arab scholar at a later date. This much should suffice for now.

A Promise by Mr. ʿAbdullāh Ātham, Representative of Dr. Martyn Clarke and the Christians, to Accept Islam if he is Defeated

Below, I have reproduced the promise of the former Extra Assistant, Mr ʿAbdullāh Ātham—who is now a pensioner and a prominent personality of Amritsar—which he made in his capacity as the representative of Dr. Martyn Clarke and the Christians of Jandiala in their debate with the Muslims. He has stated quite categorically that if he is defeated through logical arguments or is shown a heavenly sign he will accept Islam.

A Copy of the Letter Written by Mr. ʿAbdullāh Ātham on 9 May 1893 from Amritsar

To Mirza Ghulam Ahmad, Chief of Qadian

In response to what you wrote in *Ḥujjatul-Islam* I declare that if you or anyone else demonstrates by any means that the Holy Quran was revealed by God and is consistent with the attributes of the Divine, that is, through a manifest miracle or conclusive logical arguments, I will become a Muslim. Keep this letter, but forgive me if I do not take out an announcement in a newspaper to this effect.

Signed
ʿAbdullāh Ātham

A *Mubāhalah* Invitation in Response to the Announcement Published by 'Abdul Ḥaq Ghaznavī

Issued on 26th Shawwāl, 1310 Hijra

I recently read an announcement by 'Abdul Ḥaq Ghaznavī, dated 26 Shawwāl, 1310 Hijra, in which he has issued a challenge of *mubāhalah* to me. So, I say to him and to all those pretended scholars and maulawīs who consider me a disbeliever that I accept this challenge and, if Allah wills, I will be in Amritsar by 3 or 4 Dhul-Qa'dah, 1310 Hijra. The date of the *mubāhalah* has been fixed as 10 Dhul-Qa'dah but may be delayed by a day in case of adverse weather or other extenuating circumstances. But, beyond this, no further delay will be permitted. The *mubāhalah* will take place at the Eid Gah close to the Khān Bahādur Muḥammad Shāh Mosque. Owing to my morning engagement with the Christians, with whom I am to enter into a twelve day debate over the truth of Islam, all those who consider me a heretic and wish to challenge me in a *mubāhalah* should know that I will be free from 2 o' clock in the afternoon until evening. Thus, either on 10 Dhul-Qa'dah or, in case of a delay, 11 Dhul-Qa'dah, 1310 Hijra, my opponents may enter into a *mubāhalah* with me. 10 Dhul-Qa'dah has been decided on so that the other ulema who, despite the common strands of our faith, consider me a disbeliever— even though I profess the Kalima and pray facing the

Qiblah, may also have a chance to participate. Among them are Muḥiyuddīn of Lakhū; Maulawī ʿAbdul Jabbār Sahib; Shaikh Muḥammad Ḥussain Batālwī; Munshī Saʿdullāh, teacher at High School Ludhiana; ʿAbdul ʿAzīz, Wāʿiẓ, of Ludhiana; Munshī Muḥammad ʿUmar, former civil servant, Ludhiana; Maulawī Muḥammad Ḥasan Sahib, a chief of Ludhiana; Miāń Nadhīr Ḥussain Sahib of Delhi; Pīr Ḥaider Shāh Sahib; Ḥāfiẓ ʿAbdul Mannān of Wazirabad; Miāń ʿAbdullāh Tonkī; Maulawī Ghulām Dastagīr of Kasur; Maulawī Shāh Dīn Sahib; Maulawī Mushtāq Aḥmad Sahib, teacher at High School Ludhiana; Maulawī Rashīd Aḥmad Gangūhī; Maulawī Muḥammad ʿAli, Wāʿiz, of Boprāń, district Gujranwala; Maulawī Muḥammad Isḥāq and Suleimān, of Patiala; Ẓahūr-ul-Ḥasan, Sajjādah Nashīn, of Batala; and Maulawī Muḥammad, employee of Karīm Bukhsh Printing Press.

However, if any of them should baulk at taking part in the *mubāhalah*, upon reading the announcement that has been sent to them through registered post, their demurral will suffice to show that they are false and unjust in their edicts of disbelief. Foremost among them is Shaikh Muḥammad Ḥussain Batālwī the writer of *Ishāʿatus-Sunnah*. He is the most obligated to come to Amritsar on the proposed date and take part in the *mubāhalah*, for he too has asked me to enter into a *mubāhalah* with him. Let it be known that I will not take up such challenges time and time again. A *mubāhalah* is not a trivial business which can be entered into lightly. This matter should be decided once and for all. Thus, whosoever demurs after reading this advertisement and eschews this challenge will have no right in the future to issue a *mubāhalah* and may shamelessly call me what he wills from the shadows. Thus, to precipitate the denouement of this affair numerous copies of this announcement will be sent by registered post so that my opponents will have no cause for excuse. Afterwards, if they neither take part in the *mubāhalah* nor desist from calling me a disbeliever it will signal the end of the affair. Finally, I wish to say that before the *mubāhalah* takes place it will be within my rights to deliver before the gathered audience an exegesis on why I am a Muslim to those who treat me as a disbeliever.

Peace be on those who follow guidance.

Announced by
Mirza Ghulam Ahmad
30 Shawwāl, 1310 Hijra

Conclusion: If Shaikh Muḥammad Ḥussain Batālwī does not participate in the *mubāhalah* of 10 Dhul-Qa'dah. 1310 Hijra, then it will be decided that the prophecy concerning him, i.e., that he will repent of having called me a disbeliever, has been fulfilled. In the end I pray to God with the words:

O' my Lord! Curse those who do evil, transgress and make

mischief, and humiliate with defeat those who do not enter this *mubāhalah*, which has been agreed upon in terms of its time and place, and do not repent of calling me a disbeliever nor seek penance for their evil deeds. Āmīn.*

O Ye who reject me, come unto that which God and His Messenger[sa] have prescribed for the silencing of disbelievers. But if you should turn away, know that the curse of God befalls the disbelievers whose fear and retreat is testimony to their falsehood.

Mirza Ghulam Ahmad of Qadian

---

* All those ulema who declare me a disbeliever are invited to Amritsar on 10 Dhul-Qa'dah, 1310 Hijra, to enter into a *mubāhalah* challenge with me. [Author]

www.ingramcontent.com/pod-product-compliance
Lightning Source LLC
Chambersburg PA
CBHW071550080526
44588CB00011B/1863